T0042036

Be a Friend

—PEERspective on Autism—

A book providing perspective on autism
and teaching others to be a friend through
Acceptance ★ Kindness ★ Empathy

Jennifer M. Schmidt, MEd
Sara Woolf Anderson, MEd

Illustrations by Nika Venturini

Be a Friend, PEERspective on Autism

All marketing and publishing rights guaranteed to and reserved by:

FUTURE HORIZONS

817•277•0727 | Fax: 817•277•2270

www.FHautism.com | info@FHautism.com

Text © 2024 Jennifer M. Schmidt & Sara Woolf Anderson

Illustrations © 2024 Nika Venturini

All rights reserved.

No part of this product may be reproduced in any manner whatsoever without written permission of Future Horizons, except in the case of brief quotations embodied in reviews.

ISBN: 978-1-957984-70-4

— Dedication —

To our children: Elyse and Corinne, and Evie, Claire, and Ian.

— Acknowledgments —

Publishing a book is no easy task, but we are grateful to the many people who have helped us or otherwise inspired us through this process!

As mothers ourselves, we want to thank our children for showing us the unique way each child sees the world. Thank you to our husbands for supporting us as we worked on this project we are passionate about, one that can truly help all amazing students both with and without autism. This is why we became educators—sharing the values of acceptance, kindness, and empathy with others. We would also be remiss if we did not thank the students we have taught over our combined 40+ years in the classroom for inspiring the PEERspective approach.

Thank you to our early readers who helped shape this book into what you see today.

Finally, thank you to our publisher, Future Horizons, for their guidance and continued mission to help the world understand and celebrate autism.

According to data on Autism Spectrum Disorder from the CDC, more than 1 in every 50 children in the United States is on the autism spectrum. While autism is common, understanding autism is not innate. Through candid discussion and education, people can learn about the barriers those with autism may have to overcome, as well as the special gifts they bring to the world.

Children are often curious about others and ask questions or form assumptions about those they perceive as different in less-than-ideal ways. By introducing characteristics of autism in a manner that promotes understanding and inclusion, assumptions based on fear or confusion can be avoided, and attitudes of acceptance, kindness, and empathy can be fostered.

For those interested in connecting further with the text, a downloadable PDF that can be personalized about your loved one with autism can be found online at **bit.ly/ BeAFriendBook**. This beautifully designed resource will allow you to share authentically with others in your life about your loved one's special interests, preferred routines, and more. Consider sharing it with family members, teachers, peers, and others to help them better understand how to be a friend!

— Suggestions on How to Use This Book —

- Many classrooms invite parents in to be "mystery readers" or simply visit to read books with their children's classes. Along with (or instead of) reading a traditional book during a visit, parents of children with autism could consider reading this book to help facilitate conversation and understanding among peers. After reading, consider conducting a question-and-answer session in coordination with your child, their teacher, their special educator, and/or their therapist, as appropriate.

- Families can share this book with siblings, cousins, grandparents, neighbors, teammates, scout troops, and others to help open up dialogue, allow people of all ages to understand their child better, and promote acceptance, kindness, and empathy.

- Parents could use this book to help their child with autism better understand themselves. Reading the book together can be a shared experience that opens up a dialogue about autism, allows their child to share details about themselves, teaches them about how their brain works, and more.

- Teachers can use this book as a tool in classrooms to promote acceptance, kindness, and empathy of all peers while providing a new understanding of autistic peers. With permission from families, teachers could teach about a specific classmate's personal journey with autism. Along with reading the book, a variety of related extension activities can be found in the back to promote further exploration and understanding of the concepts discussed.

- This book, and others in the PEERspective series, can be a resource for preservice teacher training and instructional planning.

note:

There are a variety of ways to refer to people with autism. Some people prefer to be called neurodivergent, for example, while others prefer autistic, and others say a person with autism; the book reflects some of these ways of identifying. Make sure you talk to the autistic people in your life and use the language they prefer.

PEERspective means acknowledging the different ways everyone in the world thinks and learns. No two people are the same, but we all have many ways in which we are alike. All people both with and without autism want to feel included and cared for. When we act with acceptance, kindness, and empathy, we not only help others feel included, but we can also learn from them—and they can learn from us.

- **ACCEPTANCE** means we appreciate everyone for who they are and the things that make them unique.
- **KINDNESS** is the quality of being friendly and including those around us.
- **EMPATHY** is being able to understand and care about how someone else feels.

By treating others with acceptance, kindness, and empathy, we can be a friend and help to make the world a better place.

All people are unique
in the things we like and do.
No matter who you are,
there's no one just like you.

Our brains help make us different;
no brains are just the same.
Sometimes, people like music,
while others love basketball games.

7

Some brains have what's called autism,
which means they're especially unique.
Autism could make people seem different.
So, let's learn about autism; take a peek!

— About Autism —

Autism exists on a spectrum, which means there is a wide variety in how it presents; no two people with autism are exactly the same, just as no two people are exactly the same in general. People with autism may behave, communicate, interact, and learn in unique ways. Their brains are different, which allows them to see the world in unexpected and unique ways.

Throughout this book, we are going to learn about autism and how it impacts how someone may see and experience the world. Understanding ourselves and others can allow us to be kind and accepting to all.

What do you know about autism?

– Special Interests –

We all have special interests—
things we enjoy doing or talking about.
And sometimes our friends who have autism
have one interest they just can't live without!

People with autism might be especially interested in something or even have exceptional knowledge of a topic. For example, if they are interested in trains, they may like to only play with trains or be able to tell you lots of facts about trains.

You can be a good friend by understanding this is something that is important to them and supporting their interest; you could ask them a question about it to start a conversation—and remind them to ask you questions about your interests, too!

What are your special interests?

— Routines —

Routines are the way we are used to doing things—
the order we like things to go.
And while changing plans might not bother you,
for others, it can make their day domino!

Friends with autism often have specific routines. Maybe they prefer to always do the same activity, wear a similar outfit, or only eat specific types of foods. When there's a change to their routine, it can cause them to have big feelings that could be hard to handle. Even if just one thing happens that is unexpected or out of the ordinary, it can cause them to feel like things are toppling out of control—just like dominoes!

You can be a good friend by respecting their routines and understanding change may be tricky for them. As a good friend, you can stay kind and calm if changes upset them.

Do you have any routines you like to follow?

13

— Literal Thinking —

Sometimes, the meaning of things we say
is not always completely clear.
And, often, our friends with autism
believe exactly what they hear.

Communication can sometimes be challenging for people with autism. This happens because they are literal thinkers and sometimes believe exactly what they hear. However, people don't always use words in ways that mean exactly what they say. For example, when we say something is **_a piece of cake,_** this means something is really easy. But, if you were to tell someone with autism, "Last night's homework was a piece of cake!" they might really think you had a piece of cake for homework—and while that would be delicious, it probably is not true!

Our friends with autism might not pick up on hidden meanings in words, so we might need to change the way we say things. If we notice our friends are confused by something that was said, we can kindly explain it or say it again in a different way. We can also be careful with joking with autistic friends until they know us well and understand the ways we like to be funny.

Are there any words or phrases that have ever confused you?
What happened?

— Communication —

Words aren't the only way we speak to others.
We can also use body language, signs, or our eyes.
So don't give up on reaching out if it's tricky.
It can work but might take a few tries!

Sometimes, people with autism can talk just like you, while others may communicate in a different way. Some people might find it difficult to talk, while others could speak or sound differently. Some autistic friends like to repeat words or phrases, while others may use pictures, devices, or other technology to help them communicate.

Some days, they may be willing to talk and play, while other times, they may not want to talk, share, or take turns. This doesn't mean they don't like you; it might mean they prefer to be alone or need a break.

If you notice they seem interested in what you are doing, ask them if they'd like to join you, even if they have said no in the past!

You can be a friend by understanding that even though we don't all communicate in the same way, we can still find ways to get along. Just because someone may not want to play one day doesn't mean they never will—keep trying!

*How would it feel if you wanted to play
with a friend but didn't know how to ask?*

— Socializing —

Some people love meeting others.
They look straight at you and say hello.
But for others, it's not quite as easy;
instead of opening right up, they take it slow.

People with autism might not have an easy time talking to others. They may not make eye contact, and sometimes it may seem like they prefer to be alone. You may see them watching first before they are comfortable joining you.

You can be a good friend by understanding they may need some time and space before they are ready to participate in activities. Just because they don't want to join in at first doesn't mean they never will, so remember to respect their wishes, but also know you can continue to reach out and see if they want to play with you at different times. A simple "hi" in the hallways or a wave when you see them out in the community might seem small but could help them feel accepted and eventually open up.

Do you find it easy or hard to talk to other people?

— Perspective Taking —

For friends with autism, it can be tricky
to look at things a different way.

They might think things can only be black or white,
instead of realizing they can also be gray.

Being able to look at events from a different perspective means that we try to understand a situation from someone else's point of view. "Black and white thinking" refers to the fact that sometimes people see only one possibility or only look at things one way. For example, If you were given black and white paint, you would have those two options, but you also could mix them together to create a new option: gray. People with autism, however, might not originally think to mix it up; they may need encouragement to look at it a different way.

Our autistic friends may find it tricky to understand perspectives different from theirs. You may notice it's hard to change their mind. You can be a good friend to them in these situations by understanding they aren't being rude when they don't see things your way; this is just how they think. They may need to be reminded there are always different ways to look at situations.

Can you think of a time it was tricky for you to see things from a different point of view?

Why is it important to understand other's thoughts and feelings?

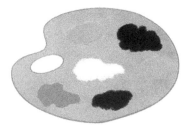

— Sensory Needs —

Sometimes, our senses aren't happy
—senses meaning things
    we smell, taste, see, hear, and feel.
And while loud noises or scratchy socks
    might not bother you,
to others, they can be a big deal.

Everyone has different sensory needs. For example, some people like tight hugs, while others prefer not to be touched. Different textures, such as tags in clothing, could also make people very uncomfortable. Some friends with autism don't like food that's too squishy or crunchy, so they eat similar foods each day. They also might use movement to help them feel calm or stay focused; they may move their body in different ways repeatedly.

Other times, some senses can be too much for people to take, so they want to avoid them; for example, they may cover their ears or wear headphones when things are too loud for them. They may even choose to avoid or limit their participation in certain activities because of their sensory needs.

You can be a good friend by understanding what others do and do not prefer and giving them space if they seem overwhelmed.

Are there any sounds, smells, tastes, or textures you like or dislike? What are they?

— Feelings —

Understanding the way others are feeling
is something our brains help us do.
But for our friends who have autism,
emotions might not be as clear as to you.

Emotions are hard for all of us to understand at times! We can learn to use body language—the faces people make and their posture—to guess what they are feeling. For example, when we see someone smiling, we can guess they are happy. For our friends with autism, though, emotions could be harder to understand.

To help friends with autism understand our feelings, we can use words to explain them when we don't think they fully understand. For example, if they have said something that makes you laugh, you could say, "Wow, that was really funny!" so they know what you are feeling and why you are laughing—and so they don't think you are laughing at them!

Expressing emotions can also be tricky. Sometimes, when we are mad, we feel like we could explode—and this happens to friends with autism, too. You might notice they don't always use their words to express their feelings but instead might show their emotions through actions. You can be a good friend in these situations by responding to the emotions that they show appropriately. If they seem excited and want to join in on something, let them! But if they seem upset, they might need some time by themselves, and that's okay, too.

*Are you usually able to tell
how someone else is feeling?
How?*

Embracing the ways we are different
makes the world more accepting and kind.
When we learn from and show empathy to others,
no one will be left behind.

27

— Extension Activities + Resources —

Special Interests:

- In the classroom, show and tell can be a fun way to spotlight students and their unique interests and talents. This can be done periodically throughout the school year and is a great way to help the students know more about each other and share their interests. In upper-level classrooms, you can even spotlight students with a Talent Showcase in place of Show and Tell.
- Help children support others' special interests by making the time to attend friends' concerts, art shows, or sporting events. Social outings are shared experiences, and shared experiences bring us closer together!
- Encourage children to make social connections with peers outside of school or in organized settings. Parents/teachers can role-play the process of asking a friend to spend time with them outside of structured activities.

Routine Based:

- Use visual schedules in the classroom or at home to help children understand what to expect. If there is a change to the routine, use a "change ahead" visual to modify the schedule.

Literal Thinking:

- To help children better understand some of the expressions they might hear others use, consider taking the time to teach idioms.
- In the classroom, pair students and assign an idiom to each group; ask them to illustrate the idiom both with its literal meaning and the way it is commonly used to show the difference between what the words mean and what people say.

Communication & Socializing:

- Teachers: if you have a student who uses sign language, consider helping your whole class learn basic sign language. What a cool skill for all students to know that will empower them to be a friend despite communication differences.

  - Conversations should go back and forth—this is a skill many young children need to practice! Practice this with a small plush toy or ball that can be used to symbolize whose turn it is to speak. The speaker holds the ball and then gently tosses the ball to a partner when it's their turn to speak. This can help all children learn conversational skills and also serve as a reminder for children with autism to remember to use reciprocity and ask their friends questions, too. Then, if you notice someone monopolizing a conversation, you can remind them to "toss the ball" as a figurative way of reminding them to share the conversation.

- Teachers: Have downtime in between classes? Intentionally plan some time to practice small talk, conversation skills, and joining in. You could teach students that if they are not sure how to start a conversation, they can use the "2 W's: weekend and weather" to pose a question to just about anyone using these two topics to get started.
- If any autistic people in your life use communication devices, consider asking a Speech and Language Pathologist (SLP)to demonstrate how their Augmentative and Alternative Communication Device (AAC) works to normalize the various ways we can communicate! For example, in the classroom, each student could introduce themselves using the AAC device or low-tech AAC core board.
- Role-playing is a fun and easy way to intentionally practice social skills and prepare for upcoming events. Remember: if you allow them to role-play what NOT to do, follow up with demonstrating the correct way!

Perspective Taking:

- While reading books aloud, pause at different points and consider asking, "How do you think the characters are feeling?" This simple question encourages children to practice perspective-taking.
- Teach your children to use "I wonder if ..." statements as an age-appropriate way to provide another perspective gently.

- Use a fun pair of glasses as a prop children can put on when trying to see things a different way. As a parent/teacher, you could model sharing your own point of view without the glasses on and then put on the glasses and share a different perspective to symbolize seeing another point of view. Children can even get in on the fun, putting on the glasses when answering questions about perspective-taking, whether with friends or in stories.

Sensory Needs:

- In schools, you could invite an occupational therapist to class to help students better understand sensory needs. For example, they could lead an exploration activity in which students try different sensory experiences to understand what they like and dislike. Perhaps they could sort items of different textures into "like" and "dislike" piles based on their sensory preferences and answer questions such as *"Do you like that? Or do you dislike it?"*

Feelings:

- Use the illustration accompanying the feelings page to identify what emotion each character might be feeling.
- Using a chart to show how someone is feeling each day can be a useful tool. This simple activity can teach them emotional regulation and give caregivers insight into where each child is starting their day. Consider having them revisit the chart later in the day to illustrate the point that it's not uncommon for moods to change throughout the day.
- Use the game charades to help children understand body language that might often be used in their environments. Teachers could model what it might look like when they are signaling for quiet versus what body language they might use when it's time to pack up, etc. This can help all students learn how to 'read the room' and interpret what is going on around them.
- Find a clip from a movie or commercial children are not familiar with. Play the clip without the sound on and ask them to guess what's happening. By watching characters' facial expressions and body language, they can practice understanding nonverbal communication and feelings.

General Ideas:

- In the classroom, use Venn Diagrams to help students understand their similarities and differences; they could be paired with a partner, or if a family provides details about their child in the fill-in templates at the end of the book, students could use the activity to identify things they have in common with their friend with autism based on the information from the student/family.

- An "All About Me" worksheet or activity could be paired with reading this book, allowing children to share about themselves and explore their own special interests, routines, etc. You also could use the template as a way to create your own version of an "All About Me" activity to show that we all have different preferences and are unique in our own ways.

- If a child with autism uses a communication device, consider inputting the template answers into their device in order to allow them to share about themselves with their peers.

- Practice charting or graphing based on interests or characteristics that are discussed in the book. For example, you could create a chart of special interests.

- Consider using role-playing scenarios to enhance understanding of specific needs and empower peers. For example, you could use scripting to help children learn how to stand up for themselves and others or prepare for an upcoming event—such as a book fair at school or an upcoming family gathering.

Supplemental Resources:

- For a middle school-targeted program and lessons for using the PEERspective Learning Approach to help preteens navigate the social world, see the book *Yes, Please Tell Me* (Schmidt & Barrett, 2021).

- To teach secondary students with autism to decode the social world using the PEERspective Learning approach, check out *Why Didn't They Just Say That?* (Schmidt, 2017). This resource provides guidance in implementing the PEERspective Learning Approach at the high-school level and is complete with lessons, activities, and more.

- For those interested in connecting further with the text, a downloadable PDF that can be personalized about your loved one with autism can be found online at **bit.ly/BeAFriendBook**. This beautifully designed resource will allow you to share authentically with others in your life about your loved one's special interests, preferred routines, and more. Consider sharing it with family members, teachers, peers, and others to help them better understand how to be a friend!

— About the Authors —

Believing the world would be a better place if people aim to practice kindness always, **Sara Woolf Anderson** is thrilled to share this book to encourage kindness, acceptance, and empathy. After graduating from the University of Notre Dame with an English degree in 2007, she has been immersed in the world of writing in various ways, working as a writer and in education, teaching hundreds of students the art of writing well. Sara lives in Dayton, Ohio, with her husband and three children.

Award-winning author and national speaker **Jennifer M. Schmidt** strongly believes that education about autism can create a more empathetic and kind environment for all students to learn and grow! With more than 25 years in the classroom, Jen continues to help students with and without autism through her innovative PEERspective Learning Approach. She teaches at Beavercreek High School and The University of Dayton, specializing in teacher training and topics related to special education. Jen lives in Beavercreek, Ohio with her husband, and she has two daughters and a son-in-law.

Printed in the USA
CPSIA information can be obtained
at www.ICGtesting.com
JSHW071719180224
57584JS00005B/11

9 781957 984704